TOOLS FOR CAREGIVERS

- **ATOS:** 0.8
- **GRL:** C
- **WORD COUNT:** 40

- **CURRICULUM CONNECTIONS:** colors, counting, textures

Skills to Teach

- **HIGH-FREQUENCY WORDS:** a, are, do, five, is, see, there, these, they, this, we, where
- **CONTENT WORDS:** clouds, color, dolphins, gray, jets, kitten, rocks, smooth, socks, wow
- **PUNCTUATION:** exclamation point, periods, question mark
- **WORD STUDY:** /f/, spelled *ph* (*dolphins*); long /a/, spelled *ay* (*gray*); long /e/, spelled *ee* (*see*); /ow/, spelled *ou* (*clouds*)
- **TEXT TYPE:** information report

Before Reading Activities

- Read the title and give a simple statement of the main idea.
- Have students "walk" though the book and talk about what they see in the pictures.
- Introduce new vocabulary by having students predict the first letter and locate the word in the text.
- Discuss any unfamiliar concepts that are in the text.

After Reading Activities

The *Let's Review!* question on page 16 asks readers to point out the gray animals they see. What other gray animals can the readers name? Do they know what sounds the animals make? Have each reader pick and draw a gray animal. Before showing their drawings to the class, ask them to make the sound of the animal. See if the other readers can guess before revealing the drawings!

Tadpole Books are published by Jump!, 5357 Penn Avenue South, Minneapolis, MN 55419, www.jumplibrary.com

Copyright ©2020 Jump. International copyright reserved in all countries. No part of this book may be reproduced in any form without written permission from the publisher.

Editor: Jenna Trnka **Designer:** Anna Peterson

Photo Credits: ZaZa Studio/Shutterstock, cover; cynoclub/iStock, 1; Efetova Anna/Shutterstock, 3 (background); Scott Hales/Dreamstime, 3 (foreground); snehrer/Shutterstock, 2tl, 4–5; guvendemir/iStock, 2ml, 6–7; Olga Popova/Shutterstock, 2br, 8–9; TungCheung/Shutterstock, 2bl, 10–11; Utekhina Anna/Shutterstock, 2mr, 12–13; elena_larina/iStock, 2tr, 14–15; Shutterstock, 16.

Library of Congress Cataloging-in-Publication Data is available at www.loc.gov or upon request from the publisher.
ISBN: 978-1-64128-934-4 (hardcover)
ISBN: 978-1-64128-935-1 (paperback)
ISBN: 978-1-64128-936-8 (ebook)

FUN WITH COLORS

GRAY

by Anna C. Peterson

TABLE OF CONTENTS

tadpole
books

WORDS TO KNOW

clouds

dolphins

jets

kitten

rocks

socks

GRAY

gray ┈┈►

Gray is a color.

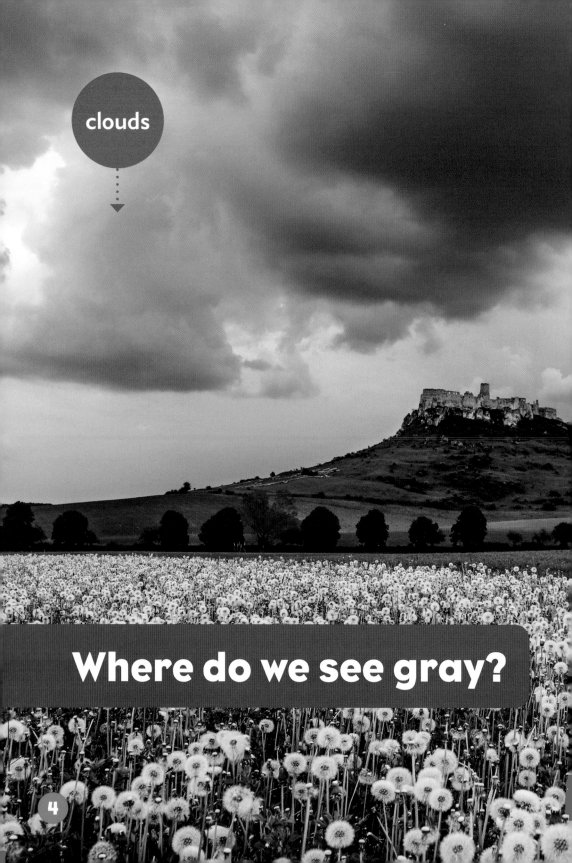

clouds

Where do we see gray?

These clouds are gray.

These jets are gray.

jet

There are five.

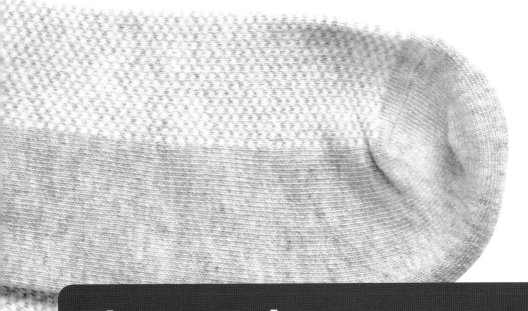

These socks are gray.

These rocks are gray.

They are smooth.

kitten

This kitten is gray.

Dolphins are gray.

dolphin

Wow!

LET'S REVIEW!

What animals are gray? Point to each gray animal you see here.

INDEX

16